CW01312696

OH BABY!

By Lottie Hulme

Copyright 2024 Lottie Hulme

All rights reserved.

ISBN: 9798884261518

DEDICATION

For Aurora Betty Altomare

I love you to the moon and back

Mummy x

CONTENTS

Part 1 - First trimester - page 8

Part 2 - Second trimester - page 24

Part 3 - Third trimester - page 43

Part 4 - Hello baby! - page 68

FOREWORD

As a professional writer, I always wanted to write a book, but I never knew what I'd write about. However, when I became pregnant at 28, I finally had my topic. I loved documenting my pregnancy over the nine months, from scribbling down notes on the tube as I made my way to work to sitting in bed with a cup of tea resting on my bump. This is a messy, unorganised, and chaotic account of the most beautiful, exciting, yet terrifying thing that ever happened to me. I didn't write this for it to fly off shelves but rather to share my little slice of reality during my first time being pregnant, in the hope that others can find sanctuary amongst the pages. Pregnancy differs for each person, and I'm by no means an expert. But perhaps somewhere between the planning, pains, and pregnancy pillows, you can find something to relate to in this little memoir. I'm writing this introduction with my beautiful baby girl, Aurora, sitting behind me in her car seat, and I can safely say having her has been the best thing to ever happen to me. Leaving little else to say but, enjoy! x

PART 1

FIRST TRIMESTER

OMG, I'm pregnant.

I found out I was pregnant on February 3rd, 2023, a day I'll never forget. I'm such a planner. Everything is meticulously planned, and I'm rarely seen without my hardback diary because, yes, I am still one of those people who shuns a digital diary and has to write everything down. So, as a planner, an unplanned pregnancy wasn't something I'd scheduled into my 2023 to-do list... Now, sitting here with my baby girl next to me, enjoying a cup of tea with some Netflix in the background, I can't imagine a world without her. It's the best thing I've ever done, and I couldn't be happier.

So how did it all begin? Well, the night before, I was at a training event for the London Marathon, which I was due to run in April 2023. When I got home from central London, I felt more exhausted than usual. But I thought nothing of it.

The next day, with a day off, I remember chilling out with my dog Luna and watching some Netflix. I was due to go out that evening with my best friend Livi and some other pals in Earlsfield. But I felt that weird exhaustion feeling again. While normally I'd put it down to my period being due, this time I knew there was a chance I could be pregnant, so I decided to do a test. I went to Co-op and bought a cheap pack of two, thinking nothing of it. I then peed on the stick as you do and left it on the floor in the lounge while I made my lunch. I remember checking it and seeing a faint second line. This had actually happened to me before - not pregnancy, but a faint second line. I googled it at the time, and it told me it was an evaporation line. Because it was so faint, I just put it down to that. But something told me it'd be worth doing a second test, just in case. So I did. The second test returned a very similar appearance, but this time the faint second line was slightly darker. I think this was the point where I started to think, 'Ok, I could be pregnant.'

Off I went to Waitrose, the big dog! And I bought a couple more tests, some cheap and some of the expensive Clear Blue electric ones that tell you how far along you are. After downing water and taking pregnancy tests like they were going out of fashion, I was left with one very clear result: Pregnant.

It was the Clear Blue test that made me realise just what was happening. I'd left it on the bathroom floor and closed my eyes as the timer flashed, preparing the result and a new future. It wasn't long before the word 'pregnant' was glaring back at me, along with the number of weeks. My initial feeling was shock, but a happy shock. Having children was something I'd always wanted. I've always wanted quite a few and to have a big family. But at this moment in time, I hadn't expected it to happen, especially given the fact that Stefano and I hadn't been together for long at all. So, while I was ecstatic on one hand, I was also worried on the other and didn't know what was going to happen.

I called my mum and told her, and I remember very little from that conversation as I was in a lot of shock. She was calm and reassuring, and I think she was excited, even though she tried not to show it as she didn't know what was going to happen either. It's all a bit of a blur. I was thinking about how I'd tell Stefano, and I knew I wanted to do it sooner rather than later, but we also had no plans to see each other until Monday. So, I was going to have to wait until then to do it in person, or just do it over the phone. I went out as planned that night and couldn't help but tell my best friends. There were conversations that I won't go into, but I knew they were trying to come at it from all angles to help give me perspective. After dinner, I left the night out early and went home as I needed to just lay in bed and think about everything. I knew what I was going to do, and I think I'd known from the moment I saw the faint second line flash up on the first test. But it was a decision that was going to change not just my life but Stefano's too.

He's a family man, uncle to adorable nieces and nephews, and the nicest person I've ever met. I still pinch myself every day that Stefano walked into my life. We get on so effortlessly and have the best time whenever we're together. And he's such a wonderful and incredible dad too (spoiler alert!) After meeting him, I knew soul mates were real. I ended up telling him the morning after I found out, and fast forward a few weeks of long dog walks and deep chats, and we'd made the most exciting, terrifying decision of our lives… we were having a baby!

The First Few Weeks...

How would I describe pregnancy in the first few weeks? Well, being hungry absolutely all the time was one way to start. You wanted to eat yourself out of the house and home, and I felt like I should have had shares in fizzy sweets companies. I devoured marshmallow flumps like they were going out of fashion, and my love for fruit grew tenfold in those initial weeks. Also, give me unhealthy, carby, cheesy dishes of food any day, and no one else would get a look-in. Coffee could go away, though. That stuff made me feel physically sick - and that was coming from the world's biggest coffee lover before the baby. Alcohol was also not my friend. I knew you're not supposed to drink when you get pregnant - and I hadn't - but even just the thought of alcohol, especially red wine, made me want to vomit. It's good, though, that I'd gone off my favourite things; otherwise, the whole journey of abstinence would have been a lot harder.

One thing I didn't have, though, was morning sickness. Not at all. The only time I did throw up was in Paris when my best friend and I went away for the weekend. We ended up having matcha pancakes, and I immediately felt disgusted. I went back to the hotel room and threw up. Me and those pancakes? It was not a Matcha made in heaven.

At one point in the early weeks, Stef and I went to the pub and got Chinese on the way home, and I remember feeling tired like I'd never felt before. I was exhausted. I needed my bed, and I needed it fast. Aside from that, I hadn't really struggled that much. It was a pretty easy ride to begin with, just involving a bit of extra sleeping and a lot more eating!

First Appointment

Even though pregnancy tests had confirmed I was pregnant, I was still constantly thinking it was too good to be true in those first few weeks, and I wanted to put my mind at rest. So, I booked something called a reassurance scan about fifteen minutes away from where I live. I didn't tell anyone I was going, and I went on a Saturday morning. On my way there, I was so excited at the prospect of seeing my baby girl for the first time. I knew there'd barely be anything to see - I had one of those tracking apps on my phone that shows the baby as the size of a peanut and so on - but I was excited nonetheless. I was so nervous lying there waiting. The sonographer put the gel on my tummy and rubbed the probe over it, and the silence felt like it was going on forever. Eventually, she told me there was a baby and a heartbeat, and I felt so overwhelmed with joy. She even printed me out a little picture, and I remember sending it to everyone, even though you couldn't see what you were looking at at all. It was just a blob. But it was the best blob I'd ever seen in my life. For me, that's when it all started to sink in a little bit more.

Eight Weeks

At eight weeks, I attended my first midwife appointment, and I felt like an intruder. I was waiting to have a general chat about pregnancy, and as I sat in the waiting room with a cup of tea and a Paperchase pregnancy diary, I literally felt like I had imposter syndrome, as if I wasn't meant to be there. Pregnancy happened so easily for me. Not that we were trying, but if we were, it would've happened pretty much straight away, and I know how rare that is. I felt amazed and so lucky that I was able to get pregnant like that, and I think for that reason, I experienced some weird imposter syndrome during the first trimester, especially partnered with the fact that we hadn't been planning on having a baby when we did.

The first appointment was straightforward and reassuring, and I had a lovely midwife named Bhav. She ended up being someone who would be there the day I went into labour, and she was with me for the whole pregnancy. We got on so well, and she made me feel at ease from the outset. I definitely overshared during that first appointment and went into how we hadn't planned to have a baby and how I felt totally out of my depth. But she was so reassuring and made it all seem like a walk in the park. I'd struck gold. Queen Mary's became a hospital I'd know like the back of my hand, as it's where I ventured for all my midwife appointments. And that's something you don't get told either - just how many midwife appointments you end up having. They were so helpful, don't get me wrong, and I'd always go with a big old list of questions prepared, but at points, it felt like I was back and forth like a yo-yo.

11 Weeks

At 11 weeks, OMG, the exhaustion! I felt quite lucky up until that point in the pregnancy because I hadn't experienced any nausea. People kept telling me that the absence of nausea was a sign that I was having a boy. I had thrown up a couple of times, each episode spurred on by matcha – clearly, I didn't learn. Aside from that, I didn't feel sick or nauseous at all. What got me was the tiredness, and it struck at any moment. It wasn't your typical tiredness either. Oh, no no no, it was a knock-your-socks-off, stop-what-you're-doing-and-curl-up-into-a-ball kind of tiredness, and your eyelids were SORE! They literally burned most mornings, no matter how much sleep I was getting. I feel like the tiredness was always a part of my pregnancy, but I noticed a couple of other little things at around 11 weeks too.

I had suffered from aura migraines all my life, but I hadn't had one in three years. Then, suddenly on a Wednesday morning out of nowhere, I had one. I was annoyed because they used to be spurred on by having black coffee or drinking too much on a night out, but I was living so clean and still got one? Blame pregnancy! I was due to be working on the 6 am shift, so I had to switch on Good Morning Britain and keep an eye on it. But I switched it on, went to make a cup of tea, and suddenly Ed Balls' head started to disappear! That's what happens when I have a migraine; my vision totally goes, and I always know when it's happening because things will start to go missing and get blurry, like those funny colours you see when petrol is in a puddle. For some reason, I didn't panic as much as I normally would – maybe because I knew what was happening and what I needed to do to get rid of it. Stef looked after me, I told work, and I got straight into bed. After a good old nap and blocking out all the lights, I was as good as new by the afternoon. Luckily, that was the only migraine I had throughout the pregnancy.

Sore boobs that were overly large were a constant throughout my first trimester. I've always had naturally big boobs, but my goodness did they quadruple in size! Oh, and there was back pain. One evening, actually the same day I had my surprise migraine, I was treated to some horrendous back pain that came out of nowhere. I could barely move out of bed, and it went on for a good few days before miraculously disappearing overnight. Bizarre, this pregnancy stuff, I tell ya. But one thing's for sure, the female body is an amazing, amazing thing.

Mother's Day

Mother's Day was odd because I kept thinking, "This time next year, I'll be a mum! How will I be celebrating? Where will I be, and what will I be doing?!" My mum told me that you never love anything as much as you love your child. I couldn't wait to understand that kind of love. I had moments where I was really scared, then really excited. I wondered about the love I'd feel. What if it didn't happen right away? It was moments like Mother's Day that made me so excited to become a mum. The thought of morning tea and handmade cards with misspelt words on them. A roast for lunch at a local pub in Wimbledon, followed by bedtime cuddles. That was what I couldn't wait for. Hurry up, baby girl...

No Symptoms

So, around the 11-week mark, and for a few weeks after that, I found I had no symptoms whatsoever. It was heading towards the start of the second trimester, and I started to get concerned about the fact that I felt so energetic, less tired, and completely symptom-free. Obviously, this is how most people want to feel every day, but when you're pregnant, it rings alarm bells that something could be wrong, especially if it's your first rodeo. I was assured by those who'd been pregnant before (and the NHS website) that this was totally normal and that you actually get a burst of energy during the second trimester. They all told me to make the most of it before the tiredness hit again.

But it still felt weird.

You go from feeling really tired and exhausted all the time to just not feeling tired at all. Or you go from painful boobs to them being not painful at all. And I had no food cravings or aversions.

So, I booked in for yet another reassurance scan because I was absolutely terrified about the fact that I didn't feel pregnant in the slightest. I've always been very on the pulse when it comes to my health. If I have the smallest inkling that something is wrong, I'll check it right away. I have no shame in doing so!

At the scan, I learned that everything was, in fact, okay, and my mind was put at rest yet again. But it goes without saying that pregnancy can be such a constant worry for so many. I've never Googled so much in my life, which I'm sure isn't a good thing, and I spent so much time looking at statistics and scary things like that, which certainly didn't help either.

I'm Growing a Human

Sometimes, I would stop and think, 'OMG, I AM GROWING A HUMAN BEING INSIDE OF ME,' then just carry on with my day. It's amazing... but also really weird. We never really discuss how weird it actually is. I found the thought of there being two hearts inside my body at one time a very bizarre concept. And I was creating a brain? Another brain for someone else?! Gosh, it really freaked me out when I thought too much about it. Kinda like when you think about what's past space, and what we exist inside, and whether we're in a goldfish bowl or just characters in someone's SIMS.

12 Weeks

Right, okay. So, I have to address the disgusting taste you have in your mouth ALL THE TIME when you're pregnant. Maybe other people don't experience this, and I guess I can't complain too much as I haven't been nauseous or sick really, but there's the strongest taste, and I couldn't put my finger on what it was. But I hated it! A lot of people experience a metallic taste, but it's not that. No, I just can't describe it! And no matter what you eat or drink, or even when you brush your teeth or have mints or gum, IT'S STILL THERE! I think that's the only thing that really left a sour taste in my mouth while pregnant... excuse the pun!

12 week scan

Finally, the time had come for the twelve-week scan. For most people, this is when you see your baby for the first time - that is unless you'd booked a reassurance scan in the weeks beforehand like I had.

Stefano and I drove to Kingston Hospital for the 12-week scan, and we were super excited. Nervous too, but those exciting nerves that bounce about your tummy like butterflies.

You have to make sure you've drunk lots of water and have a full bladder, and I'd nearly forgotten to do so. I was downing water like it was going out of fashion on the way there in the car. We waited for a little while, and I think for Stef, that's when it all became a lot more real. It definitely hits you more when you're in a maternity unit surrounded by bumps and expectations.

We were eventually called in, and like the reassurance scan, everything happened so fast! I jumped on the bed, whacked my trousers down, and then the gel went on, and suddenly on the screen, you can see the baby! It's those few seconds where you're looking at the screen where you realise just how much this teeny tiny little thing the size of a fig means to you. I was so nervous waiting to see him/her on the screen and praying an image would suddenly pop up.

When it did, the biggest smile spread across my face, and Stef was smiling too. It was just the loveliest moment, something I'll remember forever. We didn't take photos or videos or anything like that; it just felt really lovely to be in the moment.

There was a heart-stopping moment when she said that I'd have to come back next week, and I couldn't work out why. She then explained it was because the size of the baby was only showing as 11 weeks, not 12, and as you have to tick off a 12-week scan, I just had to go back and make sure everything was as it should be. I was always more than happy to - the more times I got to see the little baby, the better.

She told us our baby liked to rest its head on its chest. So cute. We also heard its heart beating and got our little photos to keep at the end. I'll never forget that day - March 23rd. It was so magical. We couldn't stop laughing too because it looked like a little spanner was in one of the scan photos. We joked that it was because the baby really had thrown a spanner in the works!

12 weeks in and an itchy belly!?

I discovered that an itchy belly is a thing! I kept waking up in the night and itching my (very small) bump! I turned to Google (Dr. Google to the rescue... again) and discovered it's a thing! Who knew?! It wasn't uncomfortable itching, and I sort of got used to it. I thought at the time, if that's my main symptom, then I'll roll with it.

At this point, I was loving food way more than usual. I could not get enough. There was one day where I felt like I'd eaten the whole of every supermarket, and I STILL wasn't full. I'd have to be rolled everywhere if I carried on.

Funnily enough, the stuff I had aversions to and didn't want during pregnancy were all the things I was eating or drinking a lot of at the start. And then things I didn't like before I was pregnant, like eggs (I know, I'm weird), I was lapping up!

Pregnancy bod

Your changing body is an amazing thing during pregnancy. I absolutely loved having a bump and not having to care about what my tummy looked like. Towards the end, when it was bigger, I enjoyed dressing it up too. I just loved being pregnant and not having to worry about things like the size of my tummy.

I love fitness and working out and always prided myself on trying to maintain the same weight and stay toned. But when you're pregnant, that's definitely harder to keep up with, especially when you're tired more often than not and have a bigger belly than normal! I think it takes some adapting too. Before your bump, it just kind of looks like you've put on loads of weight because it's not obvious you're pregnant. I was already looking forward to getting my fitness on after I'd given birth.

I had such a tiny bump throughout my pregnancy. It measured what it should, but the midwives constantly commented on it. They said it was very neat, to my delight, and it did look it. I was really happy with my bump. I loved feeling it, and Stef and my dog loved cuddling up to it and resting their heads on it. It's funny how it pops up out of nowhere too. I look back at some of the pictures I took, cradling my 'bump' when there really wasn't anything there, then suddenly BOOM, you've got a bump. It just pops. Towards the end, it was absolutely massive, and I couldn't believe it was my body when I looked in the mirror.

12 week scan... take two

I was really scared of this scan for some reason. In those beginning stages, I got so nervous every time we had to go for one. But as soon as I saw the baby pop up on the screen, I could relax.

Around this time, I woke up one morning with such a strong pain in my tummy. Then it suddenly went, but it really scared me because it was the first time I'd had it happen. I also struggled with tiredness at this stage. It was probably the worst it got. I was still working out a lot, so I wondered if it was partially hindered by that. But let's face it, it was probably just symptomatic of the pregnancy. The scan went well, though, and there was nothing to worry about. Everything was looking as it should!

Paris!

I went to Paris with my best friend Livi, and what was meant to be a boozy trip to the French capital turned into something much more wholesome. Looking back at this time, it all still feels so surreal. We covered so many steps during our weekend away, and I loved feeling fit and getting fresh air. However, I remember feeling nervous—was I meant to be walking this much while pregnant?

I was trying to be one of those people who just didn't take it all very seriously and freak out over the smallest things. But in my head, it was a different story. I panicked from time to time and would overthink things. I think this was also the first time I realised I couldn't do everything I was doing before. It was all about non-alcoholic beers and hiding the '00 on my Instagram stories so nobody knew I was expecting.

We started walking past baby shops, and I was eyeing up all sorts of things. The realisation kicked in that very soon I'd be going into shops like that to get clothes for him or her. It was here that Livi, one of the baby's three godmothers, decided to give the baby the nickname 'Raz.'

Basically, we realised she was the size of a raspberry in my tummy, and we didn't know what to refer to her as—so we shortened raspberry to Raz, et voila! It was such an amazing trip, filled with herbal tea and macarons, but it was also certainly filled with uncertainty and a bit of fear about everything to come.

First Baby Bits

My mum bought the first things for my baby: some baby wipes. It just felt so surreal, yet it was starting to get very real. I was getting increasingly excited about things like going baby shopping and buying little outfits.

On my day off, I went to H&M and got her a little white dress and a pink one. Additionally, I bought her first toy from a little market in Greenwich—a rattle! There was nothing better than shopping for all the baby things. Sometimes it felt a bit overwhelming, given there's a lot to buy, but we made a big old list and ticked things off as we went.

PART 2

SECOND TRIMESTER

Bump on Show (13 weeks in)

OMG, this is when I got offered a seat on the tube without even wearing a badge. I had a badge delivered—you can get them for free and sent to your home address—but I didn't tend to wear it very often, if at all. I definitely should've worn it more!

When I got offered the seat, I was wearing quite a tight dress, to be fair, but I think my bump had officially bumped! It was pretty exciting. I didn't really feel like I was showing that much at three months, but maybe I was! I kept meaning to buy maternity clothes but didn't because I genuinely don't think it had registered that I was pregnant, and I started wondering when the reality of it would hit.

At this stage, I just couldn't wait to find out the gender. I'd always thought I'd have a little boy first, but then when I found myself pregnant, I didn't really mind either way anymore. Plus, a girl would be super cute too.

Around the three-month mark, I was finding the idea of giving up my high heels hard to adjust to. Anyone who knows me knows I live in heels. Seriously. Very rarely does a day go by when I'm not in them. But it was around the three-month mark that I went to Oxford Street and bought… (dun, dun, dun) FLATS. Yes, I actually purchased some white trainers, and they were quite nice, to be fair, but I told myself I'd wait until I was the size of Jupiter with crippling back pain before I put them on. While I was there, Stef asked his sister-in-law what gender she thought the baby was based on our scan (she's a sonographer), and she said she thought it was a girl!

13 weeks in (again)

Okay, my bump had bumped now, and I'm not going to lie, I started feeling a bit self-conscious. I don't know why! I think it's because I was in a weird stage where I was in the middle of a proper bump and a normal tummy, so it looked like I'd eaten too many pies!

I also started to feel nervous about being pregnant over the summer. Nervous but excited. Mainly because of feeling hot, but I also wondered if I'd start to get FOMO with everyone heading out and drinking, etc.

I went for a run on Easter Sunday, and it was pretty hot, and I was feeling a bit flustered, so then I thought if I'm like this now, what the heck will it be like in summer!

Week 14

Uh oh, something very annoying happened.

I went out for dinner for my best friend's birthday, and the challenge of not drinking had gone out of the window by then, simply because I didn't feel like drinking alcohol at all. Ever. Anyway, we sat in a Mexican restaurant, and I went for an iced hibiscus flower soft drink, trying to mix things up a bit and stray away from Coke all the time...

Well anyway, little did I know that there was also a tequila-based hibiscus flower cocktail kicking about on the menu too. Also iced.

I'd pointed to the one I wanted in a bid to make sure it was a soft drink... but it turned out the waiter had just scribbled down the request. When the bill came, we queried why my £3 drink was £11.50. Much to my horror, he'd served me a tequila cocktail WHICH I HAD THEN DRUNK. I was pissed off. I knew me and baby would be fine, but it was more because I'd avoided alcohol and been so well-behaved that if I was going to sneak a drink, I wouldn't have chosen that one! Anyway, the poor guy was mortified, even more so because his wife had just had a baby. I've never seen someone go as white as a ghost like that.

We ended up getting a chunk of stuff taken off our bill, and I left happy. Cheers to that?!

I was just praying the baby didn't come out with a shot glass and a sombrero!

Social media announcement

Ok, so announcing my pregnancy on social media was actually terrifying. I wanted to wait until all friends and family knew before doing the old social media post. Then when the day finally came for me to do it, I was so nervous, don't ask me why! It was a Sunday, and I was about 14 weeks when I shared my news, and it got the most lovely reception. I don't know why I thought people would march to my house with pitchforks or be pissed off! But I think because it all came as a shock to Stef and me, I knew everyone else would have that same reaction.

But you know what, it was really lovely to have it out in the open and to receive all the messages of congratulations. I posted a little picture of Luna lying down and looking at a scan of the baby, with some flowers next to it.

I'd also told work by this point - don't worry I didn't spring the news on them with a photo of my dog and a scan on Insta. But talking to work was also a hurdle that ended up not being a hurdle at all! Again, I was so nervous to tell them, but it was such a lovely conversation that felt so easy, and the whole way through the pregnancy and afterwards, they were so supportive. It was such a relief.

That's one of the weirdest things about being pregnant. Until you're ready to tell people, you're harbouring this secret that you're both so excited yet apprehensive to share.

I feel like if we'd planned the pregnancy, maybe I would have made more of a song and dance about the announcement. But I wanted to keep things as chilled as possible and not draw too much attention.

Oh hello bump!

So at 14/15 weeks, my bump really popped. It was like it happened overnight. I kind of loved it though because I started wearing figure-hugging clothing to show it off. But I did also feel a sense of self-consciousness about it too, which was really odd. I think because it's such a big body change and actually everyone stares at your bump, so I was very conscious that it was there. Also, people will just start touching your tummy. I personally don't mind it, but I know some people find it very intrusive. Hardly surprising; someone rubbing your belly does take some getting used to! I kinda loved it though.

At 14/15 weeks was when I realised that floaty dresses were my new best friend. And I started wearing my trainers. I felt tiny! Being pregnant at the time felt so nice the whole way through. I definitely preferred being heavily pregnant when I could wear floaty dresses than I think I would if I were pregnant over winter, wearing baggy clothes and jeans.

Ugh, I want a glass of wine

I was so on board with not drinking when I started my pregnancy! I never thought about the lack of big nights out or getting boozy, and it was hard because I'd come from a career where I went out to events a lot and had that more night out-y lifestyle. But in my second trimester, I started feeling FOMO! I went to a hen do and had the best time, but as I saw everyone getting progressively tipsier, I definitely wished I could've grabbed myself a glass of savvy b!! It must be because the sickness starts to mellow out after the first trimester - not that I had it - and I never did drink, but goodness gracious me did I miss it a little bit. That said, never having a hangover and feeling fresh and ready to go every day - what a feeling!

Four months in

Four months in - wow. I'd had extreme tiredness again at the start of the four-month period, and a couple of headaches, but aside from that, symptoms have been very tame and mainly non-existent. I found myself getting excited to get to bed and eat a late-night snack, whereas I used to be the TOTAL opposite and wouldn't know when to call it a night. Funny how easy it is to just make the switch, isn't it?

At this stage, my craving for sweet stuff ramped up a gear.

My bump had really popped too, and that's what I found so surreal. Sometimes I'd have thoughts that I'd never get pregnant or see myself pregnant. Almost like when you want something so much to the point where it's so surreal when it actually does happen. I'd almost convinced myself that it just wouldn't be on the cards for me. I was so shocked when I looked in the mirror, but this time there was a sizable bump there.

I did start struggling with the image - I know that's so stupid - but it made me feel a bit self-conscious and made me worry about getting back into shape. I used to scoff at celebs who'd try and snap back into shape as soon as they'd given birth, but I do care about my fitness and my figure, and I did kind of want to make sure I got myself back to a weight I was happy with, but I knew I'll probably be too knackered to do so!

Finding out the gender

I was actually so worried during this pregnancy. On a weekend at the end of April, Stef and I were together, and I told him I wanted to go for a scan, during which we could also find out the gender. We went down at 3pm to the same place I'd gone for my very first reassurance scan, where I'd confirmed my pregnancy, and we were both so excited and nervous all at once. We decided we'd get the gender in an envelope and then go back to my garden with a bottle of 'nozeco' to open it together. Just the two of us. But things didn't exactly go to plan...

These are the things people don't tell you, and the things you don't learn about in school. The baby's heartbeat was beating loud and clear, which made us both SO happy. Still, finding out the gender... we did not. I was 16 weeks, so we would've been able to see, but our naughty little cub had its legs crossed and refused to uncross them, no matter what I did.

We were sent to go for a walk, and I was told to drink something fizzy, so I downed a Lucozade, and we went for a wander. I remember it all so clearly. We stood watching a cricket match playing out on a field opposite the baby scan venue. I was crossing everything in the hope that when we went back, we'd be able to get the gender in an envelope.

After a short wait back in the room, we tried again. No luck. I felt so sad and disappointed, but at the same time so happy because I knew the baby was fine, and I knew he/she was really comfortable in the little position they'd curled up in, so my frown was soon turned upside down. And all was not lost, as we had a return appointment booked in.

We went back on a Tuesday morning, and we FINALLY found out the gender. It was the most magical and overwhelming day. We were walking back to the car quicktime, in a bid to get home as soon as possible and see what was inside. The temptation to just open it in the car was overwhelming!

I didn't really feel nervous when we were sitting there; I was just impatient to go in and see if the legs were crossed or not. I remember Cinderella was playing in the background.

Finally in the room, and the sonographer was silent as she moved the wand about. Then she told us to close our eyes, and it was at that moment I knew it was working. When she then told us that this time had been a success, I was so excited. She did say the cheeky little cub did end up closing the legs again right after she'd done it, so we'd just caught the right window.

We went home, envelope in hand. It felt like the longest drive ever from the gender scan venue to the house. And it felt like the most precious thing we'd ever been handed. We also got some additional scan photos and 4D ones too, so that was super exciting. When we got back, I sat down and watched Married At

First Sight while Stef cooked us an omelette and made tea. I can't believe we had so much patience to wait for so long!

But before he'd even finished making breakfast, we'd pulled up a seat at the table and got ready to open it. We were both so nervous, but as I began to open it, I could see pink writing, and that's when I knew. It's a girl!

I was in floods of tears – happy tears! I think because it was the moment that it all became so real, a little girl, our little girl. It was one of the happiest moments of our lives, and I'm so glad I had the chance to experience it. We were ecstatic.

Oh hey, May... and hey first kicks

I was lying in bed on my new pregnancy pillow (how it took me so long to get one I don't know - they are a DREAM!) and started reading my new baby book. It was recommended by a friend, called Your Baby Week By Week: The Ultimate Guide. I was planning on winging it but thought I could accept a little bit of help along the way so I wasn't totally unprepared. Then suddenly... little kicks! I'm absolutely sure of it. I had never felt something like that before, and I placed my hand there, feeling teeny-tiny little movements. It was adorable. I couldn't wait for it to happen again.

Two weeks went by...

I think I felt the baby kicking again a couple of weeks later, but it was so hard to tell at that point. There was one evening the week before where it seemed like definite kicks, but other times it just felt like very light movements that were so hard to differentiate. I was already feeling impatient to meet her at this point, and I just wanted to have her in my arms, bouncing her on my knee, kissing her cheeks, and watching movies together. I wanted all the cosy stuff.

Symptoms-wise, there was nothing new. I was still very tired, and my bedtime was way earlier than it used to be! But aside from that and the occasional headache, I never really struggled like I thought I could during pregnancy.

And just like that, 19 weeks!

At 19 weeks, the symptoms were pretty non-existent.

I definitely felt little kicks from time to time now, especially when lying down, so I tried to get into positions where I knew she'd kick me just so I could feel her! We went out to Battersea, and Stef bought a little outfit for her from Zara - a babygrow with a matching cream hat - so CUTE! Just walking around the newborn clothes section with him filled my heart with so much joy. We were so excited to be parents.

20-week scan

It's not often I'm left speechless, but the 20-week scan saw me lost for words. It was incredible. For the first time, we really got a good look at our baby's profile - her beautiful little features, her tiny toes, legs, head, all of it.

The sonographer pointed out the nostrils and said the eyes were above it on the screen, and it took me a while to understand what I was looking at. But then I saw it all of a sudden, and oh my god. It was incredible. I think Stef was lost for words too.

It was a longer scan than the others as she checked all sorts of things on the screen - all of which came back positive, which felt like the biggest relief. She also confirmed that she was definitely a girl.

I could watch my baby in my tummy forever. I found it fascinating, and every time was never long enough! We were told that she was very active, and at one point, she even did a hilarious yoga pose, which the sonographer managed to catch a photo of. It was the first time bubba wasn't called stubborn too - she's learning, I guess?

At the scans, sometimes to make the baby move, you have to raise your hips up and wiggle them side to side before slamming your body down onto the bed several times to get the baby to move. I always found it so awkward. But it was worth the bum wriggle in the end.

Maternity Leave Forms

When the time came to fill in my maternity leave forms and sift through the paperwork, it dawned on me that there's a reason they say kids are expensive. Perhaps I should've grasped that sooner, right?

Trying to determine how much time I'd take felt confusing. Never having had a baby before, I was in the dark about how it would all play out – whether I'd need an extended break or if I'd be eager to dive back into work. Being intensely career-minded and passionate about my job, I worried that too much time away might not be the best idea. Yet, the idea of some family time and quality moments with my newborn was equally exciting. After working non-stop since the age of 15, was it finally time for a brief pause?

In the end, I opted for a ten-month hiatus. I can't quite pinpoint why, but it just felt like the right decision. Maternity leave, I reckon, is something you can only truly figure out once you've had the baby. Who knows, I might even find myself heading back to work earlier than planned.

21 Weeks

This week, I found myself a bit mentally scattered. Throughout my pregnancy, I hadn't really experienced the rollercoaster of hormonal ups and downs, but now, inexplicably, tears seemed to flow incessantly. I felt fortunate and content that everything was progressing well, yet I couldn't shake this emotional turmoil.

This has always been my greatest worry since becoming pregnant – the overwhelming emotions and uncontrollable tears. You tell yourself you'll manage it, have certain coping mechanisms, but when it hits, it feels like an avalanche of emotions that you can't rein in.

What made it more challenging was not initially living with Stef. On the good days, it was manageable, but on the bad days, I just yearned for someone by my side to reassure me, tell me it's okay, or simply hold my hand.

Stef was nothing short of incredible during the pregnancy, a constant pillar of support. I felt his emotional backing throughout, and he was genuinely excited about becoming a dad.

However, during weeks like this one, I found myself yearning for Stef's constant presence. I felt a heightened sense of dependence and neediness.

22 Weeks... and the Bump Was Bumping

At 22 weeks, my bump was unmistakable! Walking into a pub with a friend, I overheard someone saying, 'She's pregnant,' and it brought me immense joy. Yes, indeed, I was! Not much else changed during this period. The emotional rollercoaster from the 21st week had subsided, showcasing how swiftly things evolve week by week in pregnancy.

I sailed through this time without many side effects, enjoying significantly more energy than the challenging first trimester. I felt like my normal self, albeit with a noticeably larger belly.

Dealing with body image became a slight challenge, and I found myself pondering whether I could reclaim my pre-pregnancy physique. While determined to try, the reality of caring for a baby added an unknown layer to the journey.

Surprisingly, I hadn't used the 'I'm pregnant' excuse to bow out of events or social functions at this point. I guess I hadn't felt the need to, aiming to maintain as much normalcy in my life as possible. The notion of dramatic life changes due to impending parenthood remained distant.

As for the famed pregnancy glow, people insisted I had it, but I couldn't quite discern it myself. Regardless, I felt amazing during pregnancy, relishing the overall positive sense. Yet, there were inevitable days when I felt colossal, warm, and uncomfortable. LOL!

Feeling Kicks

One of the most enchanting moments of my pregnancy occurred when Stef felt the kicks. Around five months into the journey, the kicks were becoming stronger every day, but Stef hadn't experienced them yet. Then, during one evening, as our baby was lively, we lay on the bed. Stef put his head on my tummy and used his hand to rest against me. I guided it to where I felt the kicking, and he felt it! It was an incredibly magical moment, almost as if our baby was moving for him. A memory etched forever in my heart.

Week 24

Surprisingly, being pregnant didn't dominate my life as much as I thought it would. I continued my daily routine, occasionally forgetting I was pregnant until those little kicks reminded me. People around me were the ones frequently acknowledging my pregnancy, commenting on the bump or asking questions, which I didn't mind at all. In fact, I found joy in discussing it.

Around this time, I noticed an increase in nighttime bathroom visits. While I thought frequent urination was only a sign early in pregnancy, it persisted throughout. Nights rarely passed without waking up for a bathroom trip. It became more noticeable during the day, especially at work or social outings. Finding a restroom became a priority, something I wasn't accustomed to doing before pregnancy.

A peculiar fear of the unknown crept in—a feeling of living in a different universe. It was challenging to articulate, almost like experiencing pregnancy imposter syndrome. At 24 weeks, days seemed to be speeding by. I embarked on my first flight while pregnant, travelling to my friends' wedding in Jersey. The experience was absolutely fine, and I felt normal. Although the urge to pee was persistent, being in the window seat took some willpower. I navigated airport security, wearing my 'baby on board' badge for the added safety of flying and bustling around airports.

Preggers at a wedding

Being pregnant at a wedding proved to be quite challenging, I must admit. The day unfolded in all its breathtaking beauty, with my friend Lavie eliciting tears of joy as she gracefully walked down the aisle, looking absolutely ethereal. The reception, set in a picturesque vineyard in Jersey, was equally enchanting.

However, amidst the celebration, all I could think about was craving a glass of wine.

The weather couldn't have been more perfect—a radiant sun in a cloudless blue sky, people gathered on the grass in their floral frocks, sipping Pimms, and a joyous and carefree atmosphere permeated through the guests as we entered the venue to indulge in the feast and festivities. Seated beside another expectant mother, I found solace in the company of fellow pregnant guests, and our conversations naturally gravitated towards bumps and babies. Yet, I couldn't help but feel a twinge of envy watching my friends engage in drinking games, succumbing to fits of laughter as their merriment heightened. It was a genuine struggle for me.

I want to clarify that it's not about dependence on alcohol, but rather the reality of weddings being lengthy affairs. Navigating through the day with a diet limited to lemonade and water left my energy levels ebbing. Despite the challenges, I wholeheartedly participated—danced, revelled, and stayed up into the late hours. By bedtime, exhaustion took over, and I drifted into a deep slumber. A note to myself for the future—perhaps avoid being pregnant during the wedding season (though the likelihood is practically impossible)!

Picking Out a Name

I can't pinpoint a specific moment when we decided on our baby's name. I always had a list of names on my phone, and the top two contenders—Aurora and Arthur—remained unchanged over the years. I was drawn to the celestial sound of Aurora, perhaps influenced by my experience of seeing the Aurora Borealis in Iceland. The name means "dawn" in Latin, and, combined with Stefano's surname Altomare, loosely translated to "dawn of the high seas," a concept I found incredibly beautiful.

Surprisingly, I didn't know Aurora was the name of Sleeping Beauty, but discovering it only strengthened my choice, as I have a deep affinity for the film Maleficent. The subtle connections between Maleficent and Sleeping Beauty added more reasons to choose the name. Interestingly, there was a subliminal lion theme throughout my pregnancy. It began during a trip to South Africa in January, where I bought a lion toy for Stef, inspired by the safari theme. Watching The Lion King afterward, I realised that Aurora had 'ror' in it, sounding like 'roar,' which further connected to lions. Humorously, these lion references played a role in our decision.

We settled on Aurora quite quickly, as Stef also liked it. I was thrilled to have chosen a name well in advance, knowing for months what we would name her. While we briefly considered other names, including Mia, Aurora remained the clear choice. I also chose her middle name after my grandma—Betty. Thus, Aurora Betty Altomare was the chosen name, and we eagerly anticipated meeting her.

Week 25

OMG, I was craving sponges! Bet that wasn't a sentence you ever thought you'd read. Yep, I was one of those people. I couldn't believe it. It started when

I was at the beach in Jersey, and I had such an urge to eat the sand, and I suddenly thought, oh great, my pregnancy craving is effing sand. But then it extended to sponges, or the thought of sucking them - don't worry, I did nothing of the aforementioned, but it's definitely something I had to talk to my midwife about. I read online that it's something called pica, which could mean I have an iron deficiency. Either way, I felt like a bit of a weirdo.

I actually then had a midwife appointment and didn't ask her about it because I was a big old scaredy cat! I should've just brought it up, but there was a student midwife there, so I thought I'd save the embarrassment for one person and not two. It was so nice hearing the heartbeat again, though. I recorded it, and apparently, you can get that put into a cuddly toy. So cute. I am definitely going to be basic and do that. I started to think of signing up for pregnancy classes too. All the things you say you're not going to do when you're pregnant, you end up doing! What's next? A cast of my pregnant tummy? Watch this space...

Moving Bump

Ah, it was so strange to witness your tummy actually moving around. I had to Google, "Is it normal for a baby to move this much in my belly?" Apparently, it was a good thing! I wondered if she'd keep me on my toes this much when she was born. Probably! We were seated at Wimbledon, watching the tennis, and I showed Stef and my friend Heidi my tummy moving all over the place. Their different reactions made me laugh. Stef was loving it, while Heidi was mortified! I can't lie, I felt both at points. It's such a unique feeling, but I just felt incredibly lucky that I got to experience it in my lifetime. Gosh, I couldn't wait to meet my baby girl.

PART 3

THIRD TRIMESTER

Third Trimester Time!

I'd entered the third trimester - ah!! The tiredness was coming back, and it kind of reminded me of the first-trimester tiredness. I was falling asleep at my desk and couldn't wait to get home. Then, when I did, I was totally out of it - I went straight to bed and could barely move. My head was pounding, and I had no motivation. After a good night's sleep, though, I felt totally fine! At this point, I was really trying to rest as best as I could, and I barely had any plans, which, normally, I hate because I'm used to always being busy. However, I knew I wouldn't get time like this very often when the baby arrives, so I tried to make the most of it. I wasn't too sure when I should stop exercising. I'd been to the gym a couple of times at the start of my third trimester, but I'd stopped running by this point as I'd gotten bigger! During this time, I started to enjoy longer walks and found a new passion for walking I never used to have. It probably came at the right time too, given I'd have to push a buggy around once she was born.

Holiday with a bump

Before heading to Sardinia, I experienced an inexplicable anxiety—difficult to articulate, manifesting as occasional tightness in my chest and shortness of breath. While I felt a bit nervous about going on holiday while pregnant, excitement also bubbled within me. As a precaution, I obtained a Fit To Fly certificate from the doctor, considering I was nearing the cutoff for flying during pregnancy. Our trip, when I was about six months pregnant, turned out to be the best. We soaked up the sun, frolicked in the pool, indulged in delectable Sardinian cuisine, explored the beaches, and meandered through cobblestone streets to gather souvenirs. It was a truly romantic and beautiful experience. Sensing that this was likely our last holiday as a couple before our baby girl's arrival, we embraced every moment. Despite being pregnant, I felt the most radiant during this stage. The sun-kissed glow, the curviness of my bump, and the enlarged bosom made me understand the elusive 'pregnancy glow.' The only downsides were not being able to indulge in all the delicious food and drinks and the challenge of keeping my bump shaded when all I wanted was to bask in the sunlight. Occasionally, I reminisce about that trip and the little rock in the sea that Stef and I swam out to—it remains a beautiful memory. I dream of the day we can take our little one there.

Diabetes Test

Due to family history with diabetes, I underwent testing for gestational diabetes. The process was straightforward, but the nine-hour fasting requirement beforehand was a bit challenging! Coming from indulging in Sardinia, I landed, quickly had some lasagna with Stef, and then commenced the fasting period. Fortunately, the appointments for the check were typically super early, so I was at the hospital by 10 past 8, ready for the blood test. After that, you consume a sugary drink, somewhat reminiscent of a Capri Sun, and then patiently wait for two (yes, two) hours. I inquired about leaving and going home since I live nearby, but they preferred that I stayed or sat in the car. Surprisingly, my time in the hospital flew by, thanks to a mix of TikTok videos and managing emails and text messages. In hindsight, I definitely should've brought my laptop or a book. If I have to undergo such tests in the future, I won't make that same mistake. After another round of blood tests, I was free to go. They mentioned they would call over the next couple of days if anything was amiss, but not hearing anything meant all was good and well. At my subsequent midwife appointment, I received the reassuring news that I didn't have gestational diabetes, alleviating any concerns in that regard.

Friends feeling the bump

At 29 weeks, I went to a BBQ with some pals, and they felt the baby kicking for the first time. It was so sweet. Apart from Stef, no one had felt the kicks, so it was really nice for people I'm closest to, to experience it as well. The reactions were so funny - some of them were in awe, while others recoiled! Either way, I had a constant stream of people wanting to sit next to me so they could be right on cue whenever the next kick occurred. It was interesting that some of them had never felt a baby bump before, never mind a kick. I guess that's one of the funny perks about being the first one to be pregnant in the friendship group.

Exercise routine shifts a gear

At about 30 weeks, I decided to quit running, weightlifting, and all those activities, opting for long walks instead. I loved running so much, and I was even supposed to participate in the London Marathon a couple of months after finding out I was pregnant, but, of course, that didn't happen. So, stopping running for the time I had to was tough. It wasn't so much that I couldn't run, but more the fact that I was conscious I had a bump now, and it looked a bit funny running around Wimbledon with it. I did a lot of walking, loads, in fact. Pregnancy made me fall in love with walking. I'd walked every day with my dog Luna, but in those last weeks of pregnancy, I did even bigger walks for hours sometimes because I'd fallen in love with it so much. I did stop going to the gym on my work lunch break around this point. Now, that was something I was kind of glad about! In the latter part of my pregnancy, I had taken up barre. When I lived in Scotland during my Masters, I loved barre, so I threw myself back into it as I'd heard great things about it during pregnancy and post-partum. Aside from a few weeks before and after the baby, I didn't ever really stop barre.

Baby classes galore

Around this stage of pregnancy, it seemed like there were endless birth classes available. Our midwifery team was incredible, offering classes covering various aspects of pregnancy and childbirth, from breastfeeding to the actual delivery. I recall the classes vividly. We joined virtually, connecting with a group of other expectant parents to learn about essential topics such as nipple placement in the baby's mouth and unique techniques like 'shaking the apple tree' to induce labour— a moment that never failed to bring laughter. If you look up a photo of it, I'm sure it'll bring a smile to your face too. We found the classes to be incredibly insightful. Though we only attended two or three, Stef was particularly fascinated by the breastfeeding information. His enthusiasm in learning about it turned out to be quite beneficial for me during the actual process. He would offer guidance like 'position her like this' or 'ensure her mouth is wide enough.' Despite feeling like a novice during the classes and being somewhat out of my depth, it also strangely felt like the information would come naturally when the time arrived. I looked at the baby as a little human being, thinking that as long as her basic needs were met—food, sleep, and diaper changes—I hopefully wouldn't go far wrong.

30 weeks

As August arrived, I couldn't figure out if time was flying or moving slowly—either way, it was strange to think there were just over two months left until the baby girl would be with us. My concern during this time was how my dog Luna was going to adjust when the baby arrived. We had been trying to get her to stop sleeping on the bed, but it became challenging as that was what she was used to doing! Ideally, she would sleep outside the bedroom when the baby came, but she tended to feel left out and would pine at the door! We tried putting her in her dog bed next to our bed, and she stayed in it, but then, as soon as we were asleep, she'd jump back into bed without us realising. It was a battle. OMG, my to-do list for post-baby was so big! Things like cosmetic stuff I had been planning to do before bubba had to be postponed until after breastfeeding. Because all of this came about as a lovely surprise, I didn't cram in all my treatments! So I made a Trello board of what I wanted to achieve when the baby was here. At first, I found it daunting, but then I had a day off and realised just how much you can get done in a day. If the baby behaves herself, that is!

4D scan

The 4D scan was the most amazing day of my life. I couldn't believe it. We went down to a place in Wimbledon, and I didn't really know what to expect. I was just worried that she might not show her face, as you've really got to get the baby in the right position during the 4D scan. Upon arrival, I went through the usual routine - pulling trousers down and getting the gel on my tummy. Then, the midwife had a look around and told us the 'stubborn' baby girl was turning her head away! Typical! I thought we might have to come back for a rescan, but in the end, she managed to turn the baby around with a few prods and repositions of the wand they use. I also did some star jumps - a norm for my ultrasounds now! Anyway, when she suddenly turned it into 4D, it was mind-blowing. We saw our baby's face for the first time - her nose, which looks just like Stef's, and her little lips in a pout! She started laughing at something, sucked her fingers, and then kicked herself in the face. It was so weird to feel it and see it at the same time. I felt so close to her! I couldn't believe this was our baby that I was creating inside of me. Stef was tearing up, and I was just laying there with my mouth wide open. There was our baby girl! Of all the things I've seen in my life, this was the most amazing. Seeing her in 4D with two months to go made me even more excited to meet her. Bring on October!

Oh no, the iron's low!

Finding out I had low iron was a scary part of the whole process. It happened after my bloods came back from the diabetes check. My midwife seemed pretty shocked at just how low the levels were. To be honest, it did explain my weird desire to want to eat inedible items. I did have my suspicions that my iron might be low anyway. I started taking iron tablets and bought a ton of spinach and other foods that were good for my levels. I had been eating healthy as it is, but now I'd really upped my intake! But was it going to work? I had to wait a couple of weeks before returning for a blood test, and there we'd find out if I needed to do better.

More kicks some days than others

At 31 weeks, I experienced a bit of panic because I drank a Guinness in the hope it would help with my iron, and then I didn't feel kicks for two days. She was definitely kicking and moving, but it felt like a lot less than I was used to. So I went to the hospital for another blood test to check my iron levels. After telling them, they were quick to get me into the day assessment unit, where I was strapped to things that wrapped around me and monitored movement. I then heard the heartbeat, and my mind was instantly at ease.

I had to press a button attached to the screen every time I felt movement while wired up to the machine for twenty minutes. It was incredible of them to fit me in and be so kind and willing to test what was happening. I felt a bit silly at first because she started moving so much, and I really noticed it, but they pointed out that it was always best to check, especially as I was at 31 weeks and should be feeling her every day.

'Spongegate' continues

So I found out my iron levels hadn't improved after the first blood test, and in fact, they'd stayed exactly the same! So I went to the hospital for more. By this point, I was so used to having a needle put into my arm. I was awaiting the results for that and kept everything crossed that I didn't need an iron diffusion. It really wasn't the end of the world if I did, but for some reason, the thought of it made me really squeamish, and normally I'm not that bad.

Iron be damned!

So we got a call after another couple of weeks to go and chat with a doctor about my iron levels. We went to Kingston and sat in the same room we had for all my other appointments.

I felt so nervous, but it turns out I didn't need to be, as when we chatted with the doctor, he didn't seem concerned at all.

He advised me to take my iron tablets before I had any caffeine and said that perhaps I'd been taking them wrong.

I'd been having an Earl Grey tea around the same time I'd had my iron tablet, so I'd probably been cancelling it out, and it had stopped me from absorbing the nutrients I needed.

Instead, he advised me to drink orange juice with the tablet, and I think (from my memory) he'd told me to have it with food.

I was over the moon! I didn't have to have an infusion, and I was pretty sure I was going to be able to remember the rules surrounding my daily iron tablet.

There were no more issues with my iron levels after that, and my desire to suck on sponges soon faded...

Bump Snaps and Birth Fears

One thing I'd really recommend doing is getting some nice pictures of your bump! I went to my friend's house, and she took some lovely images of me in some of the dresses she made while cradling the bump. I did them around 31 weeks and absolutely loved the opportunity to pose for some bump photos before giving birth. I wanted them to be candid and not too pose-y, and we shot in such a beautiful space. I'll always have those photos, and that feels so special because one day I'll be able to show them to my little girl.

It was around this point when I really started to question giving birth and what it would be like. I remember calling up my mum and asking thousands of questions to try and get my head around the pain that might come with having a baby. Up until this point, I hadn't fixated on it too much, and, in fact, I wasn't really afraid at all. But then I all of a sudden began to think about it more because I knew the day was fast approaching.

32 weeks and a baby shower later...

The baby shower was complete! It honestly felt like I had organised a wedding, but the day turned out so well, and everyone had such a good time, so all the planning and running about paid off.

We had it in the garden, and there was an incredible cake baked by my friend Jess, along with balloons, shots in baby bottles, and fun games. It was such a lovely day. Stef, my best friends and our parents pulled out all the stops and put in so much effort. Times like that made me realise just how special the people in my life are. One of the baby's godmothers scattered plastic babies all over the grass and around the garden (I'm still finding them to this day!), and another organised a game where you had to guess who was who based on their baby photos. It was all so wonderful and creative, the sun was shining, and it was one of my favourite days while being pregnant, even though the lead-up had felt a bit stressful.

I felt great too. I was wearing a long patterned pink dress that I'd picked up in Sardinia, and I felt like I'd managed to secure some of that 'pregnancy glow' everyone talks about. I wore my hair down, glammed up with makeup, and got giddy on 'Nozeco.'

We had Stef's parents there, and mine, and it was so lovely for them all to spend time together. They'd also brought food they'd made, and mum hand-painted shells pink and blew up loads of balloons. We all chipped in to make it the most wonderful day ever.

Aurora is already so loved by so many people, and that felt pretty special to me. We also had a baby guest book that everyone signed, guessing her weight, time of birth, and so on. I love that we'll have that to give to her one day.

The gifts were magical too, and we got so many beautiful things from everyone that would help so much when she arrived. From little raincoats to boots, rattles, and books, no stone was left unturned, and I was overwhelmed with gratitude. It melted my heart to think of the thoughtfulness that had gone into each gift bought for her. After it, I was so ready to go into nesting mode. I just wanted to be with Stef, Luna, and the bump for a little while but decided I would keep going until the due date so I could make myself proud. Would I do another baby shower if I had another baby? Well, maybe, but definitely something more low key for the next one!

33 weeks

No major updates. I was getting pretty impatient to give birth by this point - I was just really excited to meet her and still had seven weeks to go, which felt like forever.

I also felt like I'd been 7 months pregnant for 90 years - I kept thinking when will it move to 8 months?!

The other thing we have to talk about is sex. We were still having it, which surprised me because I just didn't think we would be at that stage. But I just didn't feel very sexy - I felt really good and body confident all throughout my pregnancy, but around this point, I did feel the bump... in the way! And I knew he was trying to keep it out of his mind too when it happened. I wondered when we should stop... I guess my body would just be like okay, that's enough now?!

On another note, we really needed to sort the spare room out. I couldn't believe we hadn't started yet! But then again, I knew it was going to get done and look lovely, so I wasn't freaking out too much. We just had so much going on. A baby shower, Stef's 30th, a trip to Cornwall! We'd said that once those things were out of the way we'd go into proper baby mode... and maybe I'd get a chance to nest finally!

Packing the hospital bag

Ok, so packing my hospital bag was a daunting task for me. I felt overwhelmed, perhaps because I had been so eager to get everything right. Watching about 100 'Pack My Hospital Bag' videos on YouTube left me a bit confused about what I'd actually need.

My plan was to pack according to the recommendations on the Pampers website, as I trust their suggestions. Additionally, I chose my favourite 'pack my hospital bag with me' video and added any additional bits and bobs they recommended. Boom!

As I started packing, it genuinely got me excited. I began feeling completely fine about it because I decided to take it bit by bit over a month or so, and Stef was really helpful too!

I got the bag and little dividers (so helpful). Each of them had what I needed to pack written on them, and I made a good start by packing some of the things we'd received at the shower.

I'm a nightmare when it comes to packing—I overpack like you wouldn't believe. For example, I loaded the bag with five different 'coming home from the hospital' outfits, even though I knew I definitely wouldn't need all of them. I just love to have options.

I also threw in a ton of snacks, as if there wasn't going to be a shop or café nearby, and every single baby product that ever existed.

Other bits and bobs included 'spritz for bitz!' for... down there! I also packed nipple pads, breast pumps, formula (in case she didn't latch), a wooden comb (which I could clutch if I were in pain—I'd seen it on TikTok, obviously). I also had a book, chargers, all the things the baby might need, nappies like they were going out of fashion, a diffuser (definitely didn't need it), a speaker (definitely did need it), and her pink Aurora comforter toy along with some blankets.

I also threw in lots of spare comfy clothes for me, including pyjamas, slippers, and a dressing gown. Even though I planned on ditching the makeup for the actual birth, I still packed all of that just in case, along with a hairbrush and an Evian face spray in case I needed cooling down.

There's so much stuff I haven't included here, mainly because I'm a guilty over-packer. If I actually listed everything I ended up taking to the hospital, it would leave you in shock.

It was such a relief when the hospital bag was all packed and ready, propped up in the baby's room. But we still had a long wait on our hands...

34 weeks

As the weeks progressed, I found myself losing track of exactly how far along I was in my pregnancy. August, in particular, seemed to stretch endlessly, and I eagerly awaited the arrival of September when I could proudly declare, "I give birth next month."

The spare room, destined to become the baby's haven, was slowly transforming. Piles of boxes filled with baby essentials cluttered the space. The to-do list seemed never-ending—disposing of a bed, acquiring a sofa bed, chests of drawers, a rug, and more.

Before diving headfirst into baby preparations, we had Stef's 30th birthday to celebrate. Juggling work commitments and celebrity interviews, I suggested to Stef that we focus on his birthday first and then shift our attention to the impending baby in mid-September. The tasks ahead, from organising the spare room to finalising the hospital bag and acquiring the pram, loomed large but felt manageable.

Despite the seemingly endless checklist, we took our time, assuring ourselves that if an emergency arose, we could tackle everything in a day. It was a delicate balance between savouring the moments of pregnancy that I knew I would miss and eagerly anticipating the final month of preparation and nesting. The excitement to nest was palpable, and I couldn't wait for the last month of limbo to swiftly pass by.

35 weeks

Entering the 35th week of pregnancy brought a mix of emotions—excitement and a touch of anxiety. Time seemed to crawl, but I reminded myself that those were the last moments to enjoy certain activities before the baby's arrival.

The reality of imminent motherhood started to sink in, accompanied by both excitement and a tinge of fear. Previously confident about giving birth, I found myself growing anxious as the due date approached. Tummy cramps, though not severe, led to moments of discomfort that made me acutely aware of the potential pain awaiting during childbirth. It was a sobering realisation.

The preparation extended beyond the mental aspects, including the introduction of vaginal stretching exercises. The prospect made me uneasy, compounded by the inconvenience of having long acrylic nails that needed removal. A curious Google search on the pain of childbirth added an element of uncertainty.

As fatigue set in, I pondered whether I should have started maternity leave earlier, primarily due to mental exhaustion. The third trimester brought not only physical tiredness but also mood swings that manifested as a short fuse. While 90% of the time was filled with positivity, random bouts of irritability became a surprising and challenging side effect toward the end of the third trimester. Simple interactions could trigger unexpected agitation, highlighting the unpredictable nature of pregnancy's final stretch.

The last hurrah - A cornish babymoon

My recipe for the perfect babymoon, the last holiday before children joyfully arrive in your life forever, is simple... Enjoy some final, grown-ups only time. Take in sea views. Soak up a smattering of sunshine (British summer allowing). All with a spa treatment or two thrown in.

So that's exactly what we did.

The babymoon coincided with Stef's 30th, and it was such an incredible trip. We stayed at an adults-only hotel that gazed out over Fistral Beach. Down below, surfers bobbed up and down from dusk 'till dawn in search of waves.

During this time, I felt VERY pregnant. I was nearly ready to pop. But we really embraced the last little getaway, just the two of us.

Yes, walking was a struggle at times. We wandered across the beach and into town, and I found myself getting out of breath on more than one occasion.

Stef was also trying to wrap me up in bubble wrap and was so scared every time I walked down a step or crossed a road! It was very cute.

By this point, I was fed up with non-alcoholic drinks. I'd now moved on to virgin G&Ts in a bid to mix things up, and if I never have to have one ever again, I'll be glad.

I'd definitely recommend a babymoon to those thinking about the prospect. It's a time to make beautiful memories, just the two of you, that you can cherish for a lifetime.

36 weeks

I was happy, I was excited, but I was starting to feel a little bit frustrated. I felt like, because I'd kept going and stayed busy without any pregnancy problems, people assumed I was all fine and dandy to do everything I normally would. People were asking to meet up, go for nights out, attend events, and I loved that

I was still getting invited to things as an eight-month pregnant lady. However, I also just wanted to say... NO! I was starting to run on empty and desired to nest. I wanted to spend time at home going for long walks, organising the cupboards, or watching a movie at 2 pm with Luna! I felt like I was being pulled in a million different directions at this stage. I was due to give birth any day and felt like I hadn't even rested!

I wish I was the type of person who could just say no more easily because, if roles were reversed, I know people would say no to me if I asked them to come to nights out at 8/9 months pregnant. It was a learning curve, to say the least.

But, on the other hand, I was going to be a mum, and I wouldn't be able to do half the things for a while, so I wanted to embrace the social life and things like going into the office.

People I was pregnant at the same time as, and who had similar due dates, had started to give birth. This was a big indicator that I wasn't far behind them and that, really, it could happen any day!

Colos-what?!

You think you've got pregnancy down, and then suddenly you're introduced to colostrum harvesting! Basically, this is when you can express and collect your first milk to give to the baby when they arrive earthside. I was so surprised that I'd literally never heard of it before!

So, my midwife gave me lots of syringes, and I started to collect colostrum from my boobs to store in the freezer for when she arrived. I found it really weird at first and didn't get the hang of it straight away. From never having squeezed my boob to produce milk to having to do it to fill syringes, it was a bizarre feeling. But once I got into the swing of it, I actually really enjoyed it and felt pleased to be doing something for my baby girl that would help give her the milk she needed if she didn't latch onto the boob!

We ended up taking them to the hospital and giving them to her the first night, which was such a help when I didn't think I was giving her enough milk.

But it was one of those things that was like, what the heck? I wondered how I'd never heard of colostrum before until then! It was all such a learning curve.

It was also referred to as liquid gold, and I can see why!

37 weeks

Had a bit of a weepy one this week because we'd had the busiest of busy weekends. I'm so grateful to have the most amazing family and friends in my life, but at 37 weeks, it was like this urge descended to just close all the windows and doors, turn on Netflix, and hibernate.

To be honest, I don't think it was helped by an insanely long journey home from a 30th, after a train forgot to stop at Farringdon.

But it was on my own head because I could've just said no to going, or not gone. But I get serious FOMO! Honestly, I'm a nightmare! I just wanted to be at everything and do everything. I went to a wedding fayre to help one of my best friends with her planning. So excited to be her bridesmaid. Then after that, I knew it'd be time to strip back the diary and just relax for what was left of the pregnancy, which didn't seem to be too long given baby girl was 'engaged' with her head facing down and was ready to come at any point.

38 weeks

It felt surreal, knowing that I could give birth at any moment. I was intrigued by what the experience would feel like, though I'd probably laugh at that thought when actually in labour, thinking 'this is intense!'

We had gone through the birth plan, although it didn't take me long as I wasn't fussed about the specifics. All I knew was that I wanted an epidural if needed, especially if the pain became too much. I had also requested one of those bouncy exercise balls and noted that Stef would be my birth partner, even agreeing to cut the umbilical cord!

There were a few pain relief methods before the epidural, but one of them didn't appeal to me as it made you feel out of control of your body – a feeling I absolutely despise. Even though it might relieve a lot of pain, I preferred to skip that stage and go straight for the epidural.

Deciding when it should be my last day in the office was tricky because I could go two weeks over my due date, and then I'd have been at home for ages! There really is no guidebook for all this; I guess you just have to go by how you feel.

Also, I WAS SO EXCITED TO WEAR NORMAL CLOTHES AGAIN! Body image had been a bit of a struggle for me during pregnancy, especially as you get really big towards the end.

We attended a class with our midwives that covered labour and the different stages. It was fascinating – I couldn't believe how much there was to know.

Colostrum harvesting had become easy by this point, which delighted me. I was initially terrified about the prospect, but eventually, it just felt normal. I was producing a lot! Stef even helped me with it, which was bizarre! He must really love me, hey! I was still a little nervous about breastfeeding, but more about getting her in the right position than anything else. In our class, we learned that she'd really have to be positioned in a certain way with her mouth open to get the milk. So many things you learn along the way...

39 weeks

OMG, 39 weeks pregnant! This final stage felt like the longest and most surreal experience of my life. As I started maternity leave, it was a bit freaky, almost like going back to work after a quick holiday. Still, the excitement was undeniable, and I managed to accomplish so much. I cleared out wardrobes, organised

Luna's and the baby's stuff, prepped the baby room, treated myself to nails and a pedicure, tied up loose ends at work, and even got Halloween decorations.

Honestly, I felt like I'd been pregnant forever.

During a room tour for expecting parents, the unexpected happened—I had a sweep. For those unaware, a sweep is a procedure performed after 39 weeks to induce labour. What I thought was just a room tour turned into being on the bed with fingers up... you get the picture.

I consented to the sweep, intrigued to see if it could induce labour, but the reality took me by surprise, and I hated the feeling. They also did a swab test to check if my waters had broken, which turned out they hadn't. The midwife suggested various methods to bring on labour, including long walks, eating dates, pineapple, spicy curries, bouncing on an exercise ball, and even sex, but my energy and mood weren't up for it.

After the sweep, I experienced what I thought were contraction pains on Saturday—very mild tightening and loosening across my stomach. However, nothing happened for days after that. I got a cold, fought it off, but felt exceptionally tired and slower than usual. Despite some signs, labour seemed elusive.

To face birth head-on, I decided to lay on the sofa and watch 'One Born Every Minute.'

40 weeks... Due date and disappointment

I reached my due date on Saturday, October 14th, and I can't deny it—I felt a bit disappointed. This seemed to be a common sentiment, according to what I gathered from forums and mum groups. The due date, emphasised from the first scan, became this pivotal date around which everything revolved. When it finally arrived, and there was still no baby, it felt strangely surreal. To make the due date special, we started the day with pancakes, strawberries, cream, lemon, and sugar. We took Luna to her favourite walk around Wimbledon Common, visited our cherished pub, the Hand in Hand, for coffee, cooked a nice meal in the afternoon, and did some pumpkin carving for Halloween. The evening was spent watching Strictly and enjoying a pizza takeaway. Throughout the day, I felt relatively good, with no signs of labour. However, as midnight approached, I woke up and found myself in tears. It was a bizarre moment, feeling like I was back in lockdown, restricted and limited. I yearned to meet my little girl and kickstart the next chapter. Attempting to express colostrum earlier that day yielded no results, and I couldn't shake the disappointment. I realised I was fully prepared for her arrival and had ticked off all the necessary boxes. The next few days felt daunting, and I got emotional. Waking up, walking Luna, having lunch, taking a nap, and spending the evening on TikToks or life admin—it had only been a week since I started maternity leave, but I didn't expect to feel so lost. Despite the uncertainty, spending time with Stef and Luna was incredible—undisturbed and quality time. That's what I'll cherish when looking back at the waiting period. I longed for even the smallest sign that she'd arrive soon, whether it was a tinge in my back or the hint of contractions. No amount of dates, raspberry tea, or bouncing on the exercise ball seemed to do the trick. I'd exhausted the list and realised I needed a little something called patience.

Overdue and what to do?

I adored mornings and evenings, but afternoons turned into a puzzle of sorts. "What on earth was I meant to do now?" The days felt peculiar, a waiting game for the inevitable, but the guessing of when it would happen added a layer of uncertainty. Three days past my due date, and I couldn't help but think it wasn't surprising given the obstinate nature she'd displayed at nearly every appointment. I found myself deep into Google searches, typing things like 'overdue babies' and 'how to induce labour naturally.' The consensus? More bouncing on that exercise ball and consuming dates like they were going out of fashion. As for Netflix? Completed it. Every streaming service known to man had been conquered.

40 weeks and four days

I used to wonder why everyone had a birth story and didn't just give birth. Now I am starting to understand. At 40 weeks and four days, I attended a midwife appointment where we all shared frustration about the fact that I was still pregnant. Hearing the baby's heartbeat provided some reassurance, and then we booked my induction for Thursday (26th October), which felt surreal – having an actual date in the diary to have a baby. However, when the midwife went to feel the baby's position, she questioned whether the baby was in breach. I couldn't believe it. So, we had to go for a scan. If she was breech, I'd discuss the prospect of having a C-section. I also had to decide between two different induction options. Honestly, I now understand how this birth stuff isn't straightforward. While I always knew I'd be late, I didn't think I'd be that late and didn't think I'd need inducing. As for a C-section, I'd always been open to the possibility, which I'm glad about as it didn't come as a big shock. Leaving the appointment, I felt a bit weird, a bit anxious, and a bit disheartened, but I was going to wait and see what the scan said before deciding anything.

Baba don't breach

The scan brought good news – the baby was not in breach; in fact, she was engaged, and her head was down. It was amazing, but I also couldn't help wondering, why was she not coming then? After the appointment, we drove to see Stef's family. For the first time in a while, I felt properly distracted from all the baby stuff. It was a welcome change from sitting at home constantly thinking about it or going on dog walks just to get steps in and hopefully start labour. Staying distracted was challenging when I was so eager to meet the little one and rapidly running out of things to do!

PART 4

HELLO BABY!

Waters breaking (AT LONG LAST)

It'd been a day or so since we'd seen Stef's family, and I was getting so impatient. Mum sent Stef and me an afternoon tea delivery with scones, jam, and cream and all the trimmings, and I remember eating it and having this really lovely moment with Stef, drinking tea at the table. The sun was shining, and we felt so excited. After this, we carved a pumpkin in preparation for Halloween! Although we were having fun, I could tell we just could not wait for this baby to be born. How much longer was the wait going to go on for? Well, apparently not too long! My waters broke at half past 1 in the morning on October 21st. We were so excited! The night before we'd done everything as we normally did, had a chilled one after walking Luna, and watched some Big Brother. But I decided to try and speed things up by getting on the exercise ball for an hour and rocking backward and forwards. I also did fifty star jumps in the bedroom! Then we went to bed around 11 pm, and Stef decided to use the power of manifestation to make my waters break. We were just joking around, but he manifested that my waters would break in the early hours of the morning, and that I'd have the baby that weekend. I couldn't stop laughing when it actually happened, and my waters broke. It was the first thing I said to him - you did this! It happened when I was exactly 41 weeks pregnant, and I woke up from my sleep to discover a liquid gushing out. Not a huge amount, but a noticeable amount - noticeable enough to know that it was water breaking and nothing else. Whenever I think of what it would feel like for waters to break, I always pictured Charlotte from Sex and the City when hers breaks on the street while she's shouting at Big. I imagined it to be some big dramatic moment. It certainly wasn't like that. I woke Stef up. He didn't believe me at first! Then we called triage and let them know that I'd likely be coming in at some point. We then watched an episode of Bodies on Netflix because we had no idea what else to do and felt excited. But despite being told to wait for contractions to start, they never came. So I just went back to sleep and woke up several times throughout the night as more water broke. It started to go a pinkish colour and that alarmed me, so I asked if that was normal, as it looked like light blood. Triage told me it was. But around 5 or 6 am, there was a lot of it, and pink, so I called again, and they told me to go in. I must admit, I was panicking because it's the first time giving birth - how the heck was I really meant to know what was normal, and what wasn't? After going in, I had a brief examination, and it was confirmed that my waters had indeed broken. As expected, we were told to go home and wait for the contractions to start and enjoy what was probably our final day just the two of us! The midwife was so lovely and said to just go about the day as normal, and, of course, time the contractions and come in when it was three every ten minutes. We were due to call back at 10 pm that night if nothing had kicked off, as the likelihood was that they'd then induce labour, as they didn't tend to leave it too long once waters had broken - in case of infection. At home, I sat on the sofa while watching Netflix, sleeping, and eating all the things I love to eat. My mum and dad were coming up to stay so they could keep an eye on Luna, and the baby would likely be here the day after all being well. It all felt very surreal. I was more nervous than excited, but one thing was for sure, and that was that I was staying positive. I tried to make the whole experience as positive as possible for everyone as I wanted it to be a happy day and for no one to feel scared or stressed... even if I was secretly going crazy with fear about the pain that was yet to come. We had a Chinese takeaway that evening, and I remember my first contraction coming in the shop - McChina. I froze, as it was quite painful, and I remember thinking I can't believe I'm going to give birth in my local Chinese takeaway. Thankfully, this didn't happen. But it terrified me. Home it was to eat the food, get an early night, and see what the night held...

"PUSHHHHH"

Aurora Altomare arrived on 23rd October 2023 at 5:01 am, weighing 7 pounds 10 ounces. I couldn't quite believe she was mine. She's the cutest, most incredible baby in the world. Perfect in every way. A full head of hair, the most adorable little smile, and I love her so much it's unreal. Stefano stepped into the dad role immediately and did an amazing job. My birth journey was eventful, to say the least. My waters broke, and I was so excited. But when contractions never came, I started to understand that it wasn't going to be the easiest labour. Infection rates go up after 24 hours if your waters have broken and you're yet to go into labour, so on Saturday night at 10 pm, I called triage and explained that I'd been told to get in touch if nothing had happened. They told me to wait again, go to sleep, and if I still had no contractions then call back at 6 am. So I woke up in the morning following a night of no contractions, and that's what I did. I explained the advice I'd been given, and they told me to come in right away. We'd packed everything ready to go, my parents were up looking after Luna, and I knew it was time. I was going to have a baby. At this point, I was nervous. We drove to Kingston hospital and went into triage pretty much straight away. I got examined by someone who checked the baby's heartbeat and explained what would happen next, which was going to be the hormonal induction. It was early in the morning, and a busy time of day for them, so she told us to go for a walk and grab a coffee for an hour or so before coming back. I'll never forget that coffee. We went to Costa and wandered outside with it. It was the last time outside just having coffee, the two of us. There was a mutual understanding that our lives were about to change forever. After an hour had passed, we went back in and waited for what felt like an eternity. We sat for three hours while they found us a room, and luckily, my midwife Bhav, who has been there since the start of my pregnancy journey, was working, so she was the one to induce me. Eventually, we were taken to our room just after lunch. It was a nice room with big windows and a bathroom, and I was so glad to have a private space where we could just shut ourselves off from the world. A lot was about to happen in that room...! I remember everything so vividly from then. Bhav went for lunch, so we had an hour to get our things sorted around the space. I unpacked my fan and my pain comb and snacks and set them up around the bed and spent the rest of the hour bouncing on the exercise ball to try and get the contractions going. Eventually, Bhav returned and explained the process of the hormonal induction. At this point, I was feeling ready to kick things off but hella nervous! She also said contractions could be more painful with this kind of induction. The first thing that happened was a cannula in my hand. Which, in hindsight, was one of the worst parts of the whole process! It was put in my wrist, and honestly, I am so squeamish when it comes to things like that. I thought at the time if it was starting off this bad, how bad was it all about to get.

Then shortly after, I started to get contractions. They initially didn't feel too bad at all, and I was handling them well with no pain relief for a fair few hours, helped by bouncing on the exercise ball. I was chatting away as normal, eating snacks, and my mum and dad came to visit; everything seemed easy. And then... boom, it was like an instant change in intensity, and the contractions started to come thick and fast. I opted for some morphine and then used gas and air—let me tell you, it was the best decision ever. At this point, I was feeling okay again because I bit on the gas and air every time it started to hurt. But before long, I knew I needed the epidural. Luckily, I got it quickly, and I wasn't even nervous because the pain had gotten pretty bad, and I was more than ready. However, during the process, they hit a nerve, which is extremely rare. The worst pain shot all around my body. I quite literally jumped forward in agony and screeched. It was so painful. Luckily, they said it was common, so I wasn't too worried, and the whole process of putting the epidural in is really quick. And what a difference the epidural made! It was incredible. All the pain went, and I just felt dozy and warm. I watched Strictly while Stef watched football, and it was just an enjoyable and chilled experience. I was texting friends, laughing with Stef, and almost forgot that I was in labour. Hours and hours went by... I had another sweep, and I was gutted to hear I was still 1cm dilated. I think it was at this point that I realised a C-section was very much on the cards. It wasn't a scary concept, though, as by that point, I just wanted to meet her, whether that was a C-section or natural birth. By this point, it was about midnight, and a group of doctors came in to introduce themselves. It was a bit overwhelming because I was all of a sudden in a room with ten health professionals staring at me while watching Strictly. A lovely woman doctor spoke to me about what had been happening and the progress (or lack of). I was going to have another sweep at 4 am, so I was hoping more than anything that there would have been some progress on how much I'd dilated by then. I should add that a few hours prior, I'd been taken off the induction drip because my body had started to contract on its own without any help needed. We could also hear the heartbeat of the baby the entire time we were in the labour ward, which, in hindsight, was quite a scary thing because after midnight, we woke up to it appearing to drop at points. Anyway, after we'd met the doctors, we spent the early hours of the morning pretty much asleep. And when I woke up around 4:30 am for my sweep, everything changed.

I woke up because I felt such strong contractions in my bum. It felt odd, so heavy, and unlike the contractions I'd felt before. I was really worried because I'd had the epidural and an epidural top-up, so I couldn't understand why I was feeling pain. I panicked because I suddenly thought if I was still 1cm dilated, then I had a long way to go, and I would endure this pain throughout the process. During the evening, we'd woken up briefly to hear that the heartbeat had been a bit odd, so I just felt like everything was going wrong. The female doctor who'd spoken to me around midnight in the big group then walked in with another female colleague, and I knew she was there to tell me I needed a C-section. She still did the sweep to see how dilated I was... and I was 10cm. I couldn't believe it. I was in so much shock. How had I gone from one to 10 that fast?! Stef was asleep and woke up to hear the news, and I could tell he was just as shocked as I was. We were both baffled. The doctors were baffled. The midwife was baffled. By this point, Stef had woken up, and I was just baffled. I keep saying baffled, don't I? And didn't know what the next steps were. The doctor then told me to 'try a test push,' discreetly signalling that I was about to give birth. I was so excited but so nervous. This was the moment. I was going to give birth. I started pushing, and as I was doing so, various other people were rushing out of the room to grab the equipment and bits and pieces they needed when someone is giving birth. We were all so unprepared because it all happened so fast. The lights were low, and there was a cosy glow in the room, which made it feel pretty relaxing, which was nice. The pushing? Not so nice. I'd never practised the breathing you have to do when you're pushing out a baby, so the doctor told me I essentially needed to pretend I was doing a big poo. Lovely. I remember having to take a big deep breath in, hold it without exhaling, and push with everything I had. For a few of the pushes, I felt myself going lightheaded and nearly passing out. I was pushing so hard, and they wanted me to push even harder, and I just thought, wow, this is impossible.

But, surprisingly, I was making progress, which was aided by the fact that I was letting out the loudest noises. At one point towards the start, I screamed, and the doctor said, 'ok, let's try that again without the screaming,' and we all cracked up laughing. I remember thinking, wow, I am laughing while giving birth, that's unexpected. I also told Stef to stay where he was and not to go down to look - I am so glad I did that! Although that was a bit of a blur to me, and I don't remember it happening. Stef was incredible throughout it all. He was such a calming presence who was just beside me spurring me on, and the nurses and midwife Shannon were brilliant. I feel like I had the best team possible delivering Aurora, and everyone was positive and calm, and it didn't feel scary.

The worst bit had to be the ring of fire. People talk about it, but when it actually happens, there are no words for how intense it is. I pushed for about five minutes, and then there was one that allowed me to push Aurora's head almost out, but her body was still inside. The ring of fire is this moment when the head is crowning, and there's this horrible burning sensation. However, I couldn't push her out fully until I had another contraction. So, I was just there, waiting in absolute agony, with my legs open and what felt like 100 people waiting for me to push. It was at this point where I was just in so much discomfort, shouting 'I can't do this.' It was probably only seconds, but it felt like I had been in that position for hours. They asked me if I wanted to reach my hand down and feel the baby's head - twice! But I kept saying no; I just want her out. Finally, the contraction came, and I pushed like I'd never pushed before. I used all of my energy. That's another thing they don't tell you about the actual giving birth part - you get so thirsty! I just wanted my water; I was so thirsty it was unbelievable. Anyway, after what felt like an eternity, a lot of screaming, and a baby's head half in and half out, I finally got the contraction I was waiting for and pushed out baby Aurora. She was immediately put onto me, and I remember it so well. She was grey, making little noises but not fully crying, but after a little rub, she burst into cries, and I was so relieved to hear it. It is the most incredible, overwhelming, and surreal experience. It was perfect. And nothing brings more relief than having them safe in your arms, and you know you've done the hard part. After cuddles and skin-to-skin, all the rest seemed like a blur. Things that I deemed painful beforehand didn't seem as bad because I'd just pushed a baby out! I had to give birth to the placenta, which wasn't too bad at all, but I did find it pretty gross. Especially when they dumped it into a bucket and asked if we wanted it. I also kept banging on about the toast with butter and cup of tea we had after giving birth. It was exactly what I was craving and it arrived, and I inhaled it! And it was just the best moment ever, having my tea and toast and cradling my little baby. Unfortunately, my temperature spiked a time during the birth, and I ended up with an infection. They had to check that Aurora didn't have an infection too, so she was wheeled off with Stef, and they went to take some blood. I thought I'd want to go too, but I was so tired and delirious, and one of the midwives came in to help me get into the shower. That part was strange as there was a lot of blood, and I had to undress, and you feel like all your dignity just goes out of the window. I was also wheeling my catheter around which you have attached to you after having an epidural. There was just so much I didn't know. But I felt good; I just desperately needed sleep. After an hour or so, we were taken down to postnatal and got settled in our own room.

The baby is in the building

After giving birth, I experienced such a weird feeling of ecstasy. Everything becomes something of a blur. I vaguely remember the wheelchair arriving to wheel me to postnatal, with Aurora and Stef following behind. We had a nice private room, so I lay in the bed as soon as I got in and recovered from my infection. I felt so dizzy and out of it all day that first day. There's a lot I don't remember. Reflecting on it all now, a week later, I believe I was in a state of total shock at the birth and how everything escalated from 0 to 100 so quickly. It's a positive, but also a negative as it left me completely confused and disoriented. At the time, I thought I'm never doing that again, but now I've forgotten the pain and totally would! Funny how it works out like that...

That day, we had my parents and Stef's parents come for a visit. I remember enjoying myself and loving seeing their reactions, but I also don't remember much at all from pure tiredness. I needed to sleep for a week! But of course, you can't, because you have a baby that needs feeding. That first evening was so strange. Filled with happiness but also confusion. I didn't know how much I needed to feed her, and my milk still hadn't come through, so I stayed up all night while she cried and gave her colostrum. To be honest, I felt something like a zombie, just going through the motions.

Stef had gone home as he desperately needed a couple of hours of sleep too, but he wasn't gone for long. We ended up staying in the room until Wednesday. So I went in on Sunday and left on Wednesday. A lot longer than I expected, but then I don't even know how long I expected to be there really. It was all so new to me (which is obvious to say, seeing as I hadn't given birth before). The days we were in the hospital were a bit of a blur, and even though it's only been a few weeks, it seems like a lifetime ago now!

I did sort of enjoy it. I felt like I was in a little bubble where I could relax and get help from midwives and nurses. But at the same time, I felt so removed from the world! Stef would come in and bring me snacks and drinks from the outside world! At one point, he went and got us fish and chips, and we stank out the whole of the postnatal ward with them. We tried to sneak them in and got caught. They acted like they didn't mind, but I'm sure they did with that stench.

My parents popped in a couple of times during it too, and I went down to say goodbye to Luna outside the hospital before she headed to the New Forest for a few weeks. It was a surreal few days. It all didn't feel real. I'd wake up in the night and look at Aurora and couldn't believe she was real. She's already grown so much since then.

By Wednesday, we were absolutely itching to leave. After sitting in a chair all day breastfeeding and talking to friends and family, we eventually got discharged by our lovely midwife Bhav that evening. Getting in the car and taking Aurora home felt so surreal. I wasn't so much scared but more exhausted and a little bit stressed and ready to just unpack, watch TV, curl up on the sofa, and cuddle Rori.

Now, three weeks in—after sleepless nights, learning to breastfeed, going out for walks, introducing her to friends and family, and overall having the best time in the baby bubble—I can safely say that having a baby is the best thing I've ever done, and she's made me the happiest I've ever been. The little things don't matter anymore. She's my world, and so are Stef and Luna. I love our little family to pieces. I'm going to leave a quote below that best sums up how I feel. I've always wanted Aurora, and I feel like my dreams have come true. I'll never get over how incredibly lucky I am to have her as my daughter. And Rori, if you're ever reading this, I love you so much.

Until next time...

Endword

As 2023 ended I heard a lyric. It read: Life is what happens when you're busy making other plans.

It comes from the Lennon and Yoko Ono song Beautiful Boy (Darling Boy) and it resonated so much.

Having a baby and being a mum was something I'd always dreamt of. I thought about it all the time, but at the time I stopped thinking about it, I became pregnant and I knew it was meant to be.

At the end of the day, you can make all the plans you want for yourself, but life probably has a completely different set of plans for you.

And becoming pregnant at that exact moment may not have been planned, but it was something we both wanted, and I knew this was my time, and that having baby Aurora would be the best thing to ever happen in our lives.

She happened while I was busy making other plans, and thank goodness she did.

ENDWORD

Reflecting on my journey through pregnancy feels like flipping through the pages of a cherished diary filled with sweet and quirky anecdotes. From indulging in unexpected cravings for marshmallow flumps to a regrettable bout of morning sickness in Paris following ill-fated Matcha pancakes – an experience I vowed never to repeat – each chapter brought its own blend of surprises and delights.

Amidst the exhaustion, I found solace in the newfound luxury of sleep, breaking my personal records for hours spent in dreamland. Hosting my very first baby shower became a highlight, as friends and family gathered to celebrate the impending arrival of my little one. And then came the transformative moment of learning the art of PUSHHH, a skill I never thought I'd acquire.

Throughout this incredible journey, I became a chronicler of my experiences, scribbling down thoughts on planes, trains, and in iPhone notes as my bump expanded, and my baby, Aurora, grew within. These scribbles, a mosaic of magic and mayhem, now serve as a testament to the wild ride that pregnancy was for me.

While every pregnancy is a unique adventure, I hope that by sharing my story, others can find moments of resonance and perhaps a bit of respite. To those currently navigating the twists and turns of pregnancy, I extend my heartfelt wishes for a smooth journey. May these pages offer you a comforting companion as you kick back with a cuppa, knowing that the best is yet to come – even if it means a few sleepless nights and the inevitable growth of eye bags!

ABOUT THE AUTHOR

Lottie Hulme, a seasoned showbiz and entertainment reporter with nearly a decade of journalistic experience, has gracefully expanded her storytelling prowess beyond the glitz and glamour of the entertainment world. Following the joyous arrival of her first child, Aurora, Lottie has woven her passion for the written word into a captivating journal chronicling the profound journey of pregnancy and motherhood. With a penchant for heartfelt narratives, Lottie invites readers into her world, offering a relatable exploration of the transformative and awe-inspiring chapters of pregnancy.

Printed in Great Britain
by Amazon

e92f0a27-7e60-4c83-a3b1-75834d69f114R01